EURO-SLANG

EURO
slang

The Practical Guide to Boozing & Bonking from Mykonos to Malaga

By
ROGER HUTCHINSON

with illustrations
by EDWARD BARKER

MAINSTREAM
PUBLISHING

EDINBURGH AND LONDON

First published in Great Britain in 1992 by

MAINSTREAM PUBLISHING COMPANY (EDINBURGH) LTD
7 Albany Street
Edinburgh EH1 3UG

ISBN 1 85158 505 2

A catalogue record for this book is available from the British Library

Illustrations by Edward Barker

Typeset in New Caledonia by The Midlands Book Typesetting Company, Loughborough

Printed in Great Britain by Scotprint Ltd, Musselburgh

CONTENTS

BEFORE, DURING (AND AFTER) THE MATCH

STRAIGHT TALKING (HOW TO LOSE FRIENDS AND INFLUENCE PEOPLE)

SUN, SAND, WEATHER
(AND FINDING YOUR WAY ABOUT)

SUN, SAND, WEATHER (AND FINDING YOUR WAY ABOUT)

Where is the topless beach . . .?

FRENCH

Oú est la plage seins nus? (oo eh la plahj sehn noo?)
(*lit. trans.*)

GERMAN

Wo ist ein Oben-ohne-Strand? (vo ist ine Oben-owneh-Strand?)
(*lit. trans.*)

SPANISH

¿Dónde está la playa nudista? (donnday estah la ply-a noodeesta?)
(*lit. trans.*)

Sun, wind, and pouring cats and dogs . . .

FRENCH

Quel temps épouvantable! (kell tohmp ay-poovong-tahb-le!)
(*colloq: what lousy weather!*)

GERMAN

Was für ein mieses Wetter! (vas foor eyn meeses Vetter!)
(*colloq: what dreadful weather!*)

SPANISH

¡Qué tiempo tan malo! (kay tee-empoh tan mahloh!)
(*colloq: what lousy weather!*)

ITALIAN

Dov'é una spiaggia dove si può stare in topless? (dohvay oona spiajj-a dohvay see pu-oh staray een topless?)
(*lit. trans.*)

GREEK

Poo ine mia plaz yimnostithon?
(*lit. trans.*)

PORTUGUESE

Onde è uma praia de monokinis? (onday eh ooma praya de monokinis?)
(*lit. trans.*)

ITALIAN

Fa caldo da morire (fah kaldoh dah moor-eeray)
(*lit: it's hot enough to die*)

GREEK

Ti apesios keros!
(*lit: such awful weather!*)

Ti iperohos keros!
(*lit: great weather!*)

Sun, wind, and pouring cats and dogs . . . cont.

FRENCH

Le temps du chien!
(le tohmp doo
shee-an!)
(*colloq: it's dog's
weather!*)

Le temps du cochon!
(le tohmp doo
kosh-on!)
(*colloq: pig's weather!*)

Il pleut des
hallebardes (eel ploo
dey 'allaybard)
(*lit: it's raining
pikestaffs*)

GERMAN

Es regnet in Strömen
(ess regnet in
Stroomen)
(*colloq: it's pissing
down*)

Es ist so heiß heute
(ess ist zo hyss
hoy-te)
(*lit: it's so very hot
today*)

SPANISH

El tiempo no fue
muy católico (ell
tee-empoh no fooay
mu-wee cat-ohlico)
(*lit: the weather isn't
very Catholic, the
weather's bad*)

Hace buen tiempo
(hathay boo-en
tee-empoh)
(*lit: the weather's
good*)

Está lloviendo a
cántaros (estah
yohbiendo a cahn-
taros)
(*lit: it's raining
pitchforks*)

Está llueve chuzos
(estah looay-beh
choothos)
(*lit: it's raining darts*)

ITALIAN

Fa un freddo della
Madonna (fah
oon fredd-oh della
Madonna)
(*lit: it's cold from the
Madonna; Christ, it's
cold!*)

Che tempo horribile!
(kay tempoh orribilay!)
(*lit: what horrible
weather!*)

Che tempo splendido!
(kay tempoh
splendeedoh!)
(*lit: what wonderful
weather!*)

PORTUGUESE

Que tempo horrivel!
(kay tempoh
orreevell!)
(*lit: what horrible
weather!*)

Que tempo
maravilhoso! (kay
tempoh mara-
villoshoh!)
(*lit: marvellous
weather!*)

Está a chover (estah
a show-vair)
(*colloq: it's raining
cats and dogs*)

DUTCH

Wat een hondeweer!
(vat een hondeveer!)
(*lit: such foul
weather!*)

Wat een heerlijk
weer! (vat een
heerluke veer!)
(*lit: fantastic
weather!*)

Do you have any marijuana, can I score some grass . . .?

FRENCH

Avez-vous de la marijuana? (avvay-voo de la marijuana?)
(*lit: do you have any marijuana?*)

Le bambalouche (le bambaloosh)
(*lit: a joint of grass*)

L'herbe douce (l'erb duce)
(*lit: the sweet herb*)

Une bouffée (oon boofay)
(*lit: a puff, a joint, a reefer*)

Un drag
(*colloq: a joint*)

GERMAN

Haben Sie das marijuana? (hahben zee das marijuana?)
(*lit: do you have any marijuana?*)

SPANISH

¿Tiene la marijuana? (teeyay-ne la marijuana?)
(*lit: do you have any marijuana?*)

ITALIAN

Avete la marijuana
(avay-te la marijuana?)
(*lit: do you have any marijuana?*)

Hai da fumare?
(hayee da foom-aray?)
(*lit: do you have a smoke?*)

Maria
(*colloq: marijuana*)

Una canna (oona cah-na)
(*lit: a stick, a cane, a joint*)

Spacciare le droghe
(spatch-array lay droh-gay)
(*colloq: to push, to sell drugs*)

GREEK

Ehete i marijuana?
(*lit: do you have any marijuana?*)

PORTUGUESE

Tem a marijuana?
(*lit: do you have any marijuana?*)

Antro de fumadores
(ant-roh de foomadoresh)
(*colloq: a smoking place, an opium den*)

DUTCH

Hebt u marihuana?
(hebt oo marijuana?)
(*lit: do you have any marijuana?*)

Going to the bog, pointing Percy at the porcelain . . .

FRENCH

J'aimerais aller aux toilettes (j'aymeray allay oh twa-let)
(*lit: I must go to the toilet*)

J'aimerais aller changer son poisson d'eau (j'aymeray allay shonjay son pwa-sohng doh)
(*lit: I must go and change the fish's water*)

GERMAN

Ich muß auf die Toilette (eek mooss owf dee toilet)
(*lit: I want the toilet*)

Ich gehe mal dahin wo der Köhnig alleine hingeht (eek gaghe mal dah-hin vo der Kohnig alleyn hiyngeht)
(*lit: I go where the King goes alone*)

SPANISH

¿Dónde están los servicios? (donday estahn los serbithios?)
(*lit: where is the toilet?*)

Hacer lo que otro no puede hacer por uno (hathar lo kay ott-ro no poo-ayday hathar por oono)
(*lit: to do what nobody else can do for a chap*)

Ir a donde el rey va solo (eer a donday el ray va sohlo)
(*lit: going where the king goes alone*)

ITALIAN

Devo andare alla
toilette (dayvo
andaray alla toilet-ty)
(*lit: I'm going to the
toilet*)

Vado pisciare (vahdoh
peesh-ah-ray)
(*colloq: I'm going for
a piss*)

Vado cagare (vahdoh
cag-ah-ray)
(*colloq: I'm going for
a crap*)

GREEK

Poo ine i tooalata
(*lit: where is the
toilet?*)

PORTUGUESE

Onde são os lavabos,
o toilette, a retrete?
(onday sa'ow osh
lavabosh, o toilet, a
retraytay?)
(*lit: where are the
lavatories, the toilet,
the men's room?*)

Going to the bog, pointing Percy at the porcelain . . . cont.

SPANISH

Un mear (oon
mee-ar)
(*colloq: a piss*)

Un somorgujador
(oon somor-goohador)
(*lit: a sea diver, a
frequent urinator*)

EATING, DRINKING
(AND THE CONSEQUENCES)

EATING, DRINKING (AND THE CONSEQUENCES)

I'm starving, I could eat a horse, hungry as a hound . . .

FRENCH

Je meurs de faim (je mur de fam)
(*lit: I'm starving to death*)

J'ai l'estomac dans les talons (j'eh l'eh-stoma dohng lay talohn)
(*lit: my stomach is in my heels*)

J'ai un creux (j'eh uhn cruh)
(*lit: I have a hollow*)

Je veux bouffer des briques (je vur boofay day breek)
(*lit: I want to eat bricks, I could eat bricks*)

GERMAN

Ich sterbe vor Hunger (eek shterb-eh vor Hoonger)
(*lit: I'm very hungry*)

Ich habe einen Bärenhunger (eek hahb-eh eynen Baarenhoonger)
(*lit: I'm hungry as a bear*)

Mir Knurrt der Magen (meer nurrt der Maagen)
(*colloq: my stomach is rumbling*)

SPANISH

Me muero de hambre (mee mwero de ambray)
(*lit: I'm starving to death*)

A buen hambre no hay pan duro (a bwen ambray no ay pan doo-roh)
(*lit: there's no such thing as hard bread when you're hungry*)

Me muero de hambre canina (mee mwero de ambray kaneena)
(*colloq: I'm hungry as a dog, or I could eat dogshit*)

ITALIAN

Sto morendo di fame
(sto morendoh dee
fahmay)
(*lit: I have a great
hunger*)

Ho una fame da
lupi; mi mangerei un
bue intero (o oona
fahmay da loopi; mee
manjer-ay oon booey
een-tay-roh)
(*lit: I've the hunger of
wolves; I could eat an
entire ox*)

Ho una fame bestiale
(o oona fahmay
besty-ahlay)
(*lit: I'm hungry as a
beast*)

GREEK

Pethonos tis pinas
(*lit: I'm greatly
hungry*)

PORTUGUESE

Tenho fome (tayn-yo
fohmay)
(*lit: I'm starving*)

Estou morte de fome
(shtoo mortay de
fohmay)
(*lit: I'm dying of
hunger*)

I'm starving, I could eat a horse, hungry as a hound . . . cont.

FRENCH

Je me serrer la
ceinture (je mi serray
la senture)
(*lit: I'm tightening my
belt*)

Je danse devant le
buffet (je dohnse
devong le boofay)
(*lit: I'm dancing in
front of the snack
bar*)

ITALIAN

Ho una fame
della Madonna (o
oona fahmay della
Madonna)
(*lit: I've a hunger
straight from the
Madonna; Mother of
Jesus, I'm hungry*)

Cheers, your health, bottoms up . . .!

FRENCH

Santé! (sohngtay)
(*lit: good health!*)

Cul sec! (coo sek!)
(*lit: dry arse, dry bottom!*)

À la pomponette! (a la pomponet!)
(*colloq: toast*)

Videz vos verres! (veeday vo verr!)
(*lit: empty your glasses!*)

GERMAN

Prost! (proshd!)
(*colloq: cheers!*)

Auf dein Wohl! (owf dine Vohl!)
(*lit: to your health!*)

SPANISH

¡Salud! (salloo!)
(*lit: cheers, salute!*)

El agua es para los bueyes, el viño para los hombres (ell ag-wa ez para los boo-ayez, el veenoh para los 'ombrayz (*lit: water for oxen, wine for men*)

ITALIAN

Salute! (sa-lloo-tay!)
(*lit: cheers!*)

Cin cin! (chin chin!)
(*lit: chin chin!*)

Alla vostra!
(*lit: to you all!*)

GREEK

Stin iyia sas!
(*colloq: here's to you!*)

PORTUGUESE

À sua! (ah shooa!)
(*lit: to you!*)

DUTCH

Proost! (prohst!)
(*lit: cheers!*)

Drink, drinking, . . .

FRENCH

Laisse-toi tenter et reprends un verre (layss-twa tontay eh rayprongs uhn vair (*lit: let yourself be tempted, and have another glass*)

Il boit comme un trou (eel bwa com uhn troo) (*lit: he swallows it like a hole in the ground*)

Il boit comme un tonneau (eel bwa com uhn tonn-oh) (*lit: he swallows it like a barrel*)

GERMAN

Trinken Sie aus! (trinken zee ows!) (*colloq: drink up!*)

Was möchten Sie zu trinken? (vas mook-ten zee tzoo trinken?) (*colloq: what are you having?*)

Er ist am Ertrinken in bier (er ist am Ertrinken in beer) (*lit: he's drowning in beer*)

Er ist betrunken (*lit: he is drunk*)

SPANISH

¿Quieres un trojo? (kee-airess un tro-yo?) (*colloq: what are you having?*)

¿Que vais a tomar? (kay vays a tomar?) (*colloq: what are you all having?*)

Coger una borrachero (kok-hair oona borrachairo) (*lit: to seize a drunkenness, to go on a spree*)

Tener una merluza (tenair oona merlutha) (*lit: to have a hake, a cod, a large fish on the line, to be dragged along*)

ITALIAN

Posso offrirti qualcosa da bere? (posso off-reerty cwal-coza da bayray?)
(*lit: what can I get you to drink?*)

Finisci di bere! (finishi dee bayray!)
(*colloq: drink up!*)

È un grand bevatore (eh oon grand bevva-tory)
(*lit: he's a big drinker*)

Affoghiamo i nostri dolore in birra? (affogg-yamo ee nostree dolloray een beer-ah)
(*lit: shall we drown our sorrows in beer*)

GREEK

Boro na soo prosfero ena poto?
(*lit: can I get you a drink?*)

Pies to!
(*lit: drink up!*)

PORTUGUESE

O que bebe? (oo key beyb?)
(*lit: what are you drinking?*)

Bebam! (beybam!)
(*colloq: finish that!*)

DUTCH

Wil je iets drinken? (vil you eets drinken?)
(*lit: what are you drinking?*)

Hij is dronken (he iss dronken)
(*lit: he is drunk*)

Drink, drinking, . . . cont.

FRENCH

Il fait la nose (eel fay la noz)
(*colloq: he's hitting the bottle*)

Il est blindezingue (eel eh blahnd-ehzang-g)
(*colloq: he's pissed, he's blind drunk*)

Il a un verre dans le nez (eel a uhn vair dong le neh)
(*lit: he has a glass up his nose, he's knocking it back*)

Il est un bibard (eel eht uhn beebar)
(*colloq: he's a drunk*)

GERMAN

Um die Häuser ziehen (oom die howzer zee-en)
(*lit: to go around the houses, to go on a binge*)

SPANISH

Juerga (hoo-airga)
(*colloq: a binge*)

Nos hemos corrida la gran juerga anoche (noss-aymoss correeda la gran hoo-airga a-notchay)
(*lit: we had a great party, binge, last night*)

Nos emborrachamos a muerte (nos emborratchahmos a moo-ayrt-eh)
(*lit: we got dead drunk*)

ITALIAN

Lui è sbronzo (looee
eh sbront-zo)
(*colloq: he is pissed*)

Che sbronzatura! (kay
sbront-zatoora!)
(*colloq: what a
piss-up!*)

Drink, drinking, . . . cont.

SPANISH

Ahogó sus peñas en
vino (aho-yo soos
paynas en veenoh)
(*lit: he drowned his
pain in wine*)

Un embriagado (oon
embria-gado)
(*lit: a drunk*)

Drunk as a skunk, pissed as a newt . . .

FRENCH

Il est ivre (eel eht
eev-re)
(*lit: he is drunk*)

Il a du vent dans les
voiles (eel a doo vang
dong lay vwal)
(*lit: he has the wind
in his sails*)

Il a un coup dans
l'aile (eel a uhn coo
dong l'ay)
(*lit: he is drinking on
the wing*)

Il est bourré à zéro
(eel eh boorray a
zair-oh)
(*lit: he is full
to nothing, he's
blootered*)

GERMAN

Er ist knülle (er ist
t-nool-le)
(*colloq: he is pissed*)

Er ist breit (er ist
bry-t)
(*lit: he is wide,
broad, he is spaced
out*)

Er lallt nur noch (er
lalt noor nok)
(*lit: he can't speak
properly anymore*)

SPANISH

Se ha borracho (say
ah borratcho)
(*lit: he is pissed*)

Alzar el codo (althar
el cod-o)
(*lit: to raise the
elbow, to be drinking
hard*)

Empinar el codo
(empeenar el cod-o)
(*as above*)

Se ha grito (say a
greetoh)
(*colloq: he is high, he
is out of it*)

ITALIAN

Si è ubriaco (see eh
oobray-ah-ko)
(*lit: he is drunk*)

Si è ubriaco marcio
(see eh oobray-ah-ko
march-o)
(*lit: he is rotten
drunk*)

GREEK

Ina mathismenos
(*lit: he is drunk*)

PORTUGUESE

Està bêbado (eshtar
beybardo)
(*lit: he is drunk*)

I have a terrible hangover, a head like an anvil and a mouth like

FRENCH

J'ai une gueule de bois épouvantable (j'ay oon gewl de bwaz aypoov-ongtab-l) (*lit: I have a dreadful mouth from drinking*)

Je vois les rats bleu (je vwa lay raa bli) (*lit: I'm seeing blue rats, I have the DTs*)

Je veux tuer le ver (je vur tooay le ver) (*colloq: I need a hair of the dog*)

Hier soir, j'étais asphyxié comme un Polonais (ee-air swar, j'etays asphyxi-ay com oon Pollonay) (*lit: I was drunk as a Pole last night*)

GERMAN

Ich habe einen fürchterlichen Kater (eek habeh eyenen foorkterleeken kahter) (*lit: I have a dreadful hangover*)

Ich habe zuviel getrunken (eek hahbeh tzooveel getroonken) (*lit: I had too much to drink*)

Mein Gott, war ich gestern besoffen! (mine Got, var eek gestern besoffen!) (*lit: my God, was I pissed yesterday!*)

Einen Brummschädel haben (eyenen broomshahdel haben) (*lit: I have a buzzing head*)

SPANISH

Tengo una resaca terrible (teng-go oona resahka terr-ee-blay) (*lit: I have a terrible hangover*)

He bebido demasiado (ay beybeedo daymassyahdoh) (*lit: I drank too much*)

Tengo de goma (teng-go day gomma) (*lit: I feel like rubber*)

Tengo una papalina (teng-go oona pappaleena) (*colloq: I'm wearing a cap with earflaps, I'm deaf to the world*)

Tengo una jaqueca (tengo oona yakayka) (*lit: I have a sore head*)

a Turkish wrestler's jockstrap . . .

ITALIAN

Ho un terribile
mal di testa ('o oon
terr-ee-bilay mal dee
testa)
(*lit: I have a
dreadfully bad head*)

Ho bevuto troppo ('o
bayvooto troppo)
(*lit: I drank too
much*)

Ho passato una
notte al bianco ('o
passahto oona nottay
al biankoh)
(*lit: I spent a night
in white, I was up all
night partying*)

GREEK

Eho ena tromero
ponokefalo
(*lit: I have a bad
hangover*)

Ipia para poli
(*lit: I drank too
much*)

PORTUGUESE

Tenho dores de
cabeça (ten-yo doresh
de cabehsa)
(*lit: I have a sore
head*)

Andar a cabeça a
roda (andar a cabehsa
a rohda)
(*lit: my head is
spinning, I am dizzy*)

He's sick, he's dying, he's turned up his toes . . .

FRENCH

Évacuer le couloir
(ehvak-ooay le
koolwa)
(*lit: to empty the
passage, to be sick*)

Lâcher une fusée
(laashay oon foozay)
(*lit: to let go a burst,
to vomit*)

Aller au renard (allay
oh raynar)
(*colloq: to go to the
fox, to throw up*)

Il est parti les pieds
en avant (eel eh
partee lay pee-ayd on
avong)
(*lit: he's left with
his feet in front,
he's been carried out
dead*)

GERMAN

Ich glaube, ich muß
mich übergeben (eek
glauwbeh, eek moosh
meetch oobergehben)
(*lit: I think I'm going
to be sick*)

Ich fühle mich krank
(eek foole meetch
krank)
(*lit: I feel very
unwell*)

Er ist Abnippeln (er
ist Abnippeln)
(*colloq: he's dying,
he's cashing in his
chips*)

Er hat abgedankt
(*colloq: he has
stepped down, he's
turned up his toes*)

SPANISH

Se ha desmayado (say
ar des-myahdo)
(*lit: he has fainted*)

Está fastidiado (estar
fasteed-yahdo)
(*colloq: he's in a bad
way, he's sickening*)

No fue la comida,
sino el vino (no fooay
la comeedah, seenoh
el veenoh)
(*lit: it wasn't the
food, but the wine*)

Enferma cuando come
demasiado (enfermah
kwandoh kohmay
daymasiahdoh)
(*lit: when he eats too
much he is sick*)

ITALIAN

Rinettere (reenettayry)
(*lit: to throw back, to throw up*)

Rigettare (reejettahry)
(*lit: to reject, to vomit*)

Vomitare (vomitahry)
(*lit: to vomit*)

Sono stufo (sohnoh stoofoh)
(*colloq: I'm sick and tired*)

Morto e sotterrato (moortoh eh sottairahtoh)
(*colloq: dead as a doornail*)

GREEK

Eho tasi pros emeto
(*lit: I think I'm going to throw up*)

Petheno ya
(*lit: I'm dying*)

PORTUGUESE

Acho que vou vomitar (ashoo key voo vomitar)
(*lit: I'm going to vomit*)

Estou a morrer (shtoo ah morray)
(*lit: I am dying*)

He's sick, he's dying, he's turned up his toes . . . cont.

SPANISH

Vomitar (vomeetar)
(*lit: to vomit*)

Está profundamente
dormido (estah
profoondamentay
dormeedoh)
(*colloq: he's dead to
the world*)

Se murió de muerte
natural (say moori-oh
day mwair-tay
nattooral)
(*lit: he died a natural
death*)

ITALIAN

Profundamente
addormentato
(profoondamentay
addormentahtoh)
(*colloq: dead to the
world*)

DUTCH

Ik geloof dat moet
overgeven (eek
gehloof dat moht
overgehven
(*lit: I think that I
must throw up*)

Ik sterf (eek sterf)
(*lit: I'm dying*)

THE BIRDS AND THE BEES
(AND HOW TO GET TO KNOW THEM)

THE BIRDS AND THE BEES (AND HOW TO GET TO KNOW THEM)

He's in love, he's smitten, he's head over heels . . .

FRENCH

Il est tombé amoureux
(eel eh tombay
amoor-ou)
(*lit: he has fallen in
love*)

Il y a dans la peau
(eel ee ah donhg la
poh)
(*lit: he has it under
the skin*)

Il y a dans les
globules (eel ee ah
donhg lay gloh-bewl)
(*lit: he has it in the
corpuscles, it's got
into his blood*)

GERMAN

Er hat sich verliebt (er
hat sitch veerleebt)
(*lit: he is in love*)

SPANISH

Se ha enamorado (say
har enamorahdo)
(*lit: he is in love*)

Contigo la milpa es
rancho y el atole es
champurado (conteego
la meelpah ess
rancho ee el atolay es
champoorahdo)
(*lit: to feel like the
cornfield is an estate
and corn-drink is
champagne*)

Andar tras ella
(an-darr tra-ssel-ya)
(*lit: to chase after
her*)

ITALIAN

Si è innamorato (see
eh eenamor-ahto)
(*lit: he is in love*)

Fare il cascamorto
(fahray eel
kaskamortoh)
(*colloq: he has eyes
like a dead sheep*)

Ha occhi solo per lei
('a okhee sohloh pehr
layee)
(*colloq: he only has
eyes for her*)

È pazza de lui (ey
patsa day looey)
(*colloq: she's crazy
about him*)

GREEK

Ina erotevmonos
(*lit: he's in love*)

PORTUGUESE

Ele está apaixonado
(ellay eshtar
appashionadoh)
(*lit: he is in passion*)

Está morre de
amores (eshtar
morray day amoraysh)
(*lit: he is dying with
love*)

Está perdido de amor
(eshtar pairdeedo day
amoor)
(*lit: he is lost,
condemned, to love*)

He's in love, he's smitten, he's head over heels . . . cont.

FRENCH

Il a un pépin
pour . . . (eel ah uhn
peypan poor . . .)
(*lit: he has a kernel
for . . .*)

Il est parti sur la
bagatelle (eel eh
partay soor la
bagatelle)
(*lit: he's gone for the
trifle, the bit of stuff,
he's cuntstruck*)

She (he) is gorgeous, a nice bit of stuff, do you know her (him) . . .?

FRENCH

C'est un beau petit
lot, est-ce une amie
à vous? (set uhn bo
pettee loh, eh-seh
oon ah-mee a voo?)

GERMAN

Das ist ein geiler
Typ! (Dass ist eyn
gyler tip!)
(*colloq: that's some
chick!*)

SPANISH

Se guapa, ¿es amiga
suya? (say gwahpah,
ess ameega soo-yah?)
(*lit: she's beautiful,
is she a friend of
yours?*)

PORTUGUESE

Está vive de amor
e brisas (eshtar
veevay day amoor eh
breeshash)
(*lit: he's living on
love and bread and
cheese*)

ITALIAN

Lei è sexy, è una
tua amica? (lay eh
sexy, eh oona tooah
ameekah?)
(*lit: she is sexy, is she
a friend of yours?*)

GREEK

Ine thavmasio, ine fili
soo?
(*lit: he/she is
beautiful, do you
know her/him?*)

She (he) is gorgeous, a nice bit of stuff, do you know her (him) . . .? cont.

FRENCH

(*lit: that's a nice bit of stuff, is she a friend of yours?*)

C'est une bonne baiseuse, est-ce . . .? (set oon bon baysooz, eh-seh . . .?) (*lit: she'd be a good screw, is she . . .?*)

C'est une fille séduisante, est-ce . . .? (set oon fee saydweesongt, eh-seh . . .?) (*lit: she's seductive, is she . . .?*)

Il est sexy, est-il un ami à vous? (eel eh sexy, eht-eel uhn ah-mee a voo?) (*lit: he is sexy, is he a friend of yours?*)

GERMAN

Sie ist (er ist) sehr attractiv, wohnt sie (er) hier? (See ist (er ist) sehr attractif, vohnt see (er) heer?) (*lit: she is (he is) very attractive, is she (he) staying here?*)

Das ist eine scharfe Braut! (Dass ist eyneh scharf-eh brort!) (*lit: that's a hot broad!*)

SPANISH

Es magnifico, ¿es hospedo aqui? (ess mag-neefikoh, ess 'ospaydoh ackey? (*lit: he's gorgeous, is he staying here?*)

ITALIAN

Lui è sexy, è uno
tuo amico? (looey eh
sexy, eh oono too-oh
ameeko?)
(*lit: he is sexy, is he a
friend of yours?*)

Lei è bella come il
sole (lay eh bellah
cohmay eel solay)
(*lit: she's as beautiful
as the sun*)

Lei è bellissima (lay
eh bell-ees-simah)
(*lit: she's
extraordinarily
gorgeous*)

Che bella figa (kay
bellah feeka)
(*lit: what a great
piece of ass*)

PORTUGUESE

Ela encantador, ela
fica aqui? (aylah
enkantador, aylah fika
ackey?)
(*lit: she is terrific,
enchanting, is she
staying here?*)

Ele atraente, ele é
sua amigo? (aylay
attray-entay, aylay eh
sooah ameegoh?)
(*lit: he is very
attractive, is he a
friend?*)

Ela excitante (aylah
exceetantay)
(*lit: she is exciting*)

Ele sexy, sexualmente
(aylay sexy,
sexualmentay)
(*lit: he is sexy,
sexually attractive*)

She (he) is gorgeous, a nice bit of stuff, do you know her (him) . . .? cont.

FRENCH

Elle est une chaude
lapine (ell eht oon
showd la-ppan)
(*lit: she is a hot
rabbit*)

Elle est une poupée
(ell eht oon poopay)
(*lit: she's a doll*)

Masturbation, jerking off, beating the meat and pulling the wire . . .

FRENCH

S'en battre une (s'ong batt-roon)
(*colloq: to beat oneself*)

S'astiquer le manche (s'asstee-kay le monch)
(*lit: to polish one's own shaft*)

Épouser la veuve poignet (aypowzay la verve poyn-yet)
(*lit: to marry the widowed sleeve*)

Étrangler Popol (ày-trong-glay poppole)
(*lit: to strangle Popol*)

GERMAN

Ein wichsen (eyen viksen)
(*colloq: a wank*)

Sich einen runterholen (seek eyenen roonterholen)
(*lit: to take oneself down, to reduce oneself*)

SPANISH

Hacerse una paja (Hathair-se oona pay-ha)
(*lit: to play with the straw*)

ITALIAN

Masturbare
(mastoorba-ray)
(*lit: to masturbate*)

Si fa una pompa (see
fah oona pompa)
(*lit: to pump oneself*)

Masturbation, jerking off, beating the meat and pulling the wire . . . cont.

FRENCH

Jouer de la
mandoline (jooay de
la mandoleen)
(*lit: to play on
the mandolin, to
masturbate a woman*)

Mettre la main au
panier (mett-r la
mahnoh panyaih)
(*lit: to put one's hand
in the bread basket,
to masturbate a
woman*)

He is gay, a bender . . .

FRENCH

Il est homosexuel (eel eh-hommosessuel)
(*lit: he is homosexual*)

Il est gai (eel eh gay)
(*lit: he is gay*)

Il est de la famille tuyau de la poêle (eel eh de la fammee too-o de la pohayle)
(*lit: he is of the group with a tube in the stove*)

Il est de la bague (eel eh de la bag)
(*lit: he is fond of the ring*)

GERMAN

Er ist schwul (er ist schvool)
(*colloq: he is gay*)

Er ist verkerht herum (er ist veerkayrt heeroom)
(*lit: he is the other way round*)

Er ist vom anderen Ufer (er ist vom anderen oofer)
(*lit: he is from the other shore*)

SPANISH

Se ha un marica (say ah oon mareekah)
(*colloq: he is gay*)

Se ha un maricōn (say ah oon marikohn)
(*colloq/derogatory: he is gay, queer*)

Se ha una cajetilla (say ah oona cah-he-teelah)
(*lit: he is a packet of cigarettes, a fag*)

ITALIAN

Si è un gay (see eh
oon gay)
(*lit: he is gay*)

Si è una sodomita
(see eh oona
sodomeetah)
(*lit: he's a sodomite*)

Si è un finocchio (see
eh oon finohk-yo)
(*lit: he's a fennel
bulb*)

GREEK

Ina omofilofilos
(*lit: he is homosexual*)

PORTUGUESE

E um homosexual (eh
oom omoseshual)
(*lit: he is homosexual*)

E um fulano (eh oom
foolanoh)
(*colloq: he is gay*)

E um sujecto (eh
oom soojektoh)
(*lit: he's a subject, a
subordinate*)

DUTCH

Hij is homofiel (he is
homofeel)
(*lit: he is homophile*)

She is gay . . .

FRENCH

Elle est une lesbienne
(ell eh-toon lesbyienn)
(*lit: she is a lesbian*)

Elle est une
éplucheuse de
lentilles (ell eh-toon
ay-ploosh-ooze de
lonteel)
(*lit: she is a lentil-
peeler*)

Elle aime l'ail (ell
aim l'aye)
(*lit: she likes the
garlic clove, the
clitoris*)

GERMAN

Sie ist die Lesbierin
(see ist dee Lesbeerin)
(*lit: she is a lesbian*)

SPANISH

Se una lesbiana (say
oona lesbyahna)
(*lit: she is a lesbian*)

Se una tortillera (say
oona torteel-yera)
(*lit: she's a maker
of, an enthusiast for,
tortillas, or Spanish
omelettes*)

ITALIAN

Lei è una lesbica (lay
eh oona lesbika)
(*lit: she's a lesbian*)

GREEK

Ina mia lesvia
(*lit: she's a lesbian*)

PORTUGUESE

É uma lésbica (eh
ooma lehshbeeka)
(*lit: she's a lesbian*)

DUTCH

Zij is lesbisch (she is
lesbeesh)
(*lit: she's a lesbian*)

She is a prostitute, a street-walker . . .

FRENCH

C'est une prostituée
(set oon pro-sti-too-
ay)
(*lit: she is a prostitute*)

Elle fait l'horizontale
(ell-fay lor-ee-zon-
tahl)
(*lit: she makes her
living on her back*)

C'est une essoreuse
(set oon essor-ooze)
(*lit: she is a mangler,
a wringer*)

C'est une recoleuse
(set oon rekohl-ooze)
(*lit: she solicits for
business*)

C'est une putain (set
oon poo-ten)

GERMAN

Sie ist eine
Prostituierte (see
ist eyen-eh pros-ti-
tewerteh)
(*lit: she is a
prostitute*)

Sie ist eine Nutte
(see ist eyen-eh
nooteh)
(*colloq: she is a
whore*)

SPANISH

Se una prostituta (say
oona pro-sti-too-tah)
(*lit: she is a prostitute*)

Se una puta (say oona
pootah)
(*lit: she is a whore*)

ITALIAN

É una prostituta (eh
oona pro-sti-too-tah)
(*lit: she is a prostitute*)

É una putana (eh
oona poo-tah-na)
(*lit: she is a whore*)

GREEK

Ine mia porni
(*lit: she is a prostitute*)

PORTUGUESE

É uma prostituta (eh
ooma proshti-too-tah)
(*lit: she is a prostitute*)

É corromper (eh
cor-rompay)
(*lit: she whores, she
corrupts*)

DUTCH

Zij is een prostituee
(she is een prosti-
tuay)
(*lit: she is a prostitute*)

I love you . . .

FRENCH

Je t'aime (je temm)
(*lit: I love you*)

GERMAN

Ich liebe dich (eek
leeb-e deek)
(*lit: I love you*)

SPANISH

Te quiero (tay
ke-yairoh)
(*lit: I love you*)

ITALIAN

Ti amo (tee amoh)
(*lit: I love you*)

Ti voglio bene (tee
vohl-yoh benneh)
(*lit: I want you
madly*)

GREEK

Sagapo
(*lit: I love you*)

PORTUGUESE

Adore vai (adoray
vye)
(*lit: I love you*)

DUTCH

Ik hou van je (eek
how van you)
(*lit: I love you*)

Can I have a condom, please; do you have any French letters . . .

FRENCH

Est-ce que vous
pouvez me donner un
préservatif, s'il vous
plaît (ess-eh kuh voo
poovay meh donnay
oon pray-ser-va-teef,
seel voo play?)
(*lit: could you
give me a condom,
please?*)

As-tu une capote
anglaise? (ah-too oon
ca-poht ong-glayz?)
(*lit: have you an
English cloak?*)

GERMAN

Haben Sie ein
Kondom? (hahben
zee eyen Kondom?)
(*lit: have you a
condom?*)

Haben Sie ein
Gummi? (hahben zee
eyen Goomy?)
(*lit: have you a
rubber?*)

ITALIAN

Avete di preservative, per favore? (avaytee dee pre-sair-va-tee-vay, per fa-vo-ray?) (*lit: do you sell condoms, please?*)

GREEK

Poo boro na agoraso ena profilaktiko? (*lit: where can I buy a condom?*)

PORTUGUESE

Tem um preservativo? (tem oom preshervateevoh?) (*lit: do you have a condom?*)

Let's make love, let's screw, let's bonk . . .

FRENCH

Veux-tu faire l'amour avec moi? (vi-too fayr lahmoor avek mwa?) (*lit: would you like to make love with me?*)

Veux-tu boum du petit matin? (vi-too boom doo peh-tee matang?) (*lit: would you like to bang, party until morning?*)

Aimes-tu une partie de jambes en l'air? (emm-too oon par-tee de jomb-song lerr?) (*lit: would you like a legs-in-the-air party?*)

GERMAN

Willst du mit mir schlafen? (villst doo mitt meer schlafen?) (*lit: will you sleep with me?*)

Möchten Sie ein Ficken? (moochten zee eyen Ficken) (*lit: would you like to fuck?*)

Ich möchte gern Vogėln (eek mook-teh gern Vohgehln) (*colloq: I'd like to screw like the birds*)

SPANISH

Hagamos el amor? (*lit: would you like to make love?*)

Quisiera chingar (kee-see-ayra cheengar) (*lit: I'd like a casual, loose screw*)

Quisiera joder (kee-see-ayra johdayr) (*colloq: I'd like to fuck*)

ITALIAN

Facciamo l'amore?
(fatch-yamoh lam-
moh-ray?)
(*lit: shall we make
love?*)

Scoppiamo (skopp-
yahmoh)
(*lit: let's sweep up,
let's brush the floor*)

Ti piace fottere?
(tee pee-ah-chay
fot-tay-ray?)
(*lit: do you like
stuffing?*)

Ti piace chiavare?
(tee pee-ah-chay
kee-ah-vah-ray?)
(*lit: do you like to
turn the key in the
lock?*)

GREEK

As kanoome erota?
(*lit: would you like to
make love?*)

PORTUGUESE

Vamos fazer amor
(vammosh farzay
ammoor)
(*lit: let's go and make
love*)

Let's make love, let's screw, let's bonk . . . cont.

FRENCH

Je veux une partie
de picquet (je vi oon
par-tee de pee-kay)
(*lit: I'd like a
fence-post planting
party*)

Veux-tu baisade?
(vi-too bay-zahd?)
(*colloq: would you
like to screw?*)

Veux-tu la dérouillage?
(vi-too la day-roo-lahj?)
(*lit: would you like
derusting?*)

Aimes-tu le torpillage?
(emm-too le torpee-
yahj?)
(*lit: do you like
torpedoing?*)

FRENCH

Je veux casser la
canne (je vi cas-say la
can)
(*lit: I'd like to break
my cane*)

Je veux mettre
la cheville dans le
trou (je vi mett-r la
chevee dong le troo)
(*lit: I'd like to put my
plug in the hole*)

Cock and balls . . .

FRENCH

Le cigare à
moustache (le seegar
ah moostash)
(*lit: the moustachioed
cigar, the penis*)

L'andouille à col
roulé (lon-doo-ee ah
coll roolay)
(*lit: the sausage in a
polo-neck*)

Le petit frère (le
peh-tee frer)
(*lit: the little brother*)

Le baigneur (le
bayhn-your)
(*lit: the bather*)

Marquer midi
(markay meedee)
(*lit: to mark midday,
to have an erection*)

GERMAN

Die Schwarz (dee
Schvarts)
(*lit: the tail, the
penis*)

Ein Latte (eyen
Latteh)
(*colloq: an erection*)

Ein Rohr (eyen roar)
(*lit: a pipe, an
erection*)

Der Hoden
(*lit: the testicles*)

Der Eier (der Eyer)
(*colloq: the eggs, the
balls*)

SPANISH

Le pito (lay pee-toh)
(*lit: the car horn, the
penis*)

La polla (lah poll-yah)
(*lit: the chicken, the
hen, the penis*)

Pendejo (pen-dayc-
ho)
(*colloq: pubic hair*)

Tenerlo parado (ten-
ayr-loh par-ah-doh)
(*lit: to have something
standing, an erection*)

Los testiculos (los
testee-koo-los)
(*lit: the testicles*)

Los cojones (los
kohc-ho-ness)
(*colloq: the balls*)

ITALIAN

Il pene (eel penneh)
(*lit: the penis*)

Il cazzo (eel kat-soh)
(*colloq: the cock*)

Uccello (oo-tchel-loh)
(*colloq: a bird, the penis*)

I testicolos (ee testee-kolloss)
(*lit: the testicles*)

I palli (ee pah-lee)
(*colloq: the balls*)

I coglioni (ee kol-ye-ownay)
(*colloq: the balls*)

GREEK

Enas orhis
(*lit: the balls*)

PORTUGUESE

O penis (oh paynish)
(*lit: the penis*)

Os testiculos (osh teshtikoolosh)
(*lit: the testicles*)

DUTCH

De testikels
(*lit: the testicles*)

Cock and balls . . . cont.

FRENCH

Barbu (barboo)
(*colloq: pubic hair*)

Les testicules (lay
tes-ti-cool)
(*lit: the testicles*)

Les balloches (lay
bal-losh)
(*lit: the bollocks*)

Les bijoux de famille
(lay bee-joo de
fammee)
(*lit: the family jewels*)

Les couilles (les
cwee-yi)
(*colloq: the balls*)

Vagina, pussy, jellyroll . . .

FRENCH

J'aime ton vagin
(jemm tong vajang)
(*lit: I love your vagina*)

Une boite à ouvrage
(oon bwat ah oovrahj)
(*lit: a workbox*)

L'abricot (lab-ree-kot)
(*lit: an apricot*)

La chatte (la shatt)
(*lit: the pussy*)

Le bouton de rose (le
boo-tong de rozz)
(*lit: the rose-button,
the clitoris*)

Clicli (kleeklee)
(*colloq: the clitoris*)

Le grain de café (le
gran de ca-ffay)
(*lit: the coffee-bean,
the clitoris*)

GERMAN

Die Vagina (dee
vajeena)
(*lit: the vagina*)

SPANISH

Me encanta la
tuya vagina (mee
en-kan-tah lah too-ya
vahc-hee-nah)
(*lit: I adore your
vagina*)

La coño (lah cohn-
yoh)
(*lit: the cunt*)

La concha
(*lit: the sea-shell, the
cunt*)

La criadilla (lah
cree-ah-deel-yah)
(*lit: the little serving-
girl, the clitoris*)

La culantrillo (lah
coo-lan-treel-yoh)
(*colloq: female pubic
hair*)

ITALIAN

Adoro la tua vagina
(ah-doh-roh lah tua
vah-jee-nah)
(*lit: I adore your
vagina*)

La figa (lah fee-kah)
(*colloq: the cunt*)

GREEK

O kolpos
(*lit: the vagina*)

PORTUGUESE

Adoro a tua vagina
(*lit: I love your
vagina*)

La bainha (lah
bayn-ya)
(*colloq: the sword's
sheath*)

The arse, the ring . . .

FRENCH

L'entrée des artistes
(long-tray daze
arteest)
(*lit: the artists'
entrance*)

Le petit guichet (le
peh-tee gwee-shay)
(*lit: the little hatch*)

La boite à pâté (la
bwat ah pattay)
(*lit: the can of pâté*)

L'oeil de bronze (loy
de brongz)
(*lit: the bronze eye*)

Le cul (le coo)
(*colloq: the arse*)

La bague (la bag)
(*lit: the ring*)

GERMAN

Der Hintern
(*lit: the behind*)

Der Arsch
(*lit: the arse*)

SPANISH

Donde las espaldas
pierden su nombre
(donday las espaldas
pee-ayr-den soo
nombray)
(*lit: where the back
loses its name*)

El trasero (ell
trasayroh)
(*lit: the behind*)

El ano (ell ahnoh)
(*colloq: the anus*)

El culo (ell coo-loh)
(*colloq: the arse*)

Las posaderas (lass
posadayras)
(*colloq: the buttocks*)

ITALIAN

Il sedere (eel
say-day-ray)
(*colloq: the arse*)

GREEK

O kolos
(*lit: the arse*)

PORTUGUESE

O traseiro (oh
trashayroh)
(*lit: the backside*)

Anal sex, shirtlifting . . .

FRENCH

Je veux baiser à la riche (je vi bay-zay ah la reesh)
(*lit: I like to screw in the richness*)

Prendre de l'oignon (prongd-r de l'on-yong)
(*lit: to take the onion*)

Casser coco (kassay koko)
(*lit: to break a bloke*)

Veux-tu tourner la page? (vi-too toor-nay la pahj?)
(*lit: would you like to turn the page?*)

Tremper la soupe (trompay la soupp)
(*lit: to soak in the soup*)

GERMAN

Der Arschficken
(*lit: arsefucking*)

SPANISH

Culear (coolay-ar)
(*lit: coming from behind*)

ITALIAN

Avere rapporti
sodomitici (avay-
ray rappor-tee
sodomi-teet-chee)
(*colloq: to be of that
persuasion*)

PORTUGUESE

Entregar-se à
pederastia (ayntraygar-
shay ah pedayrast-ya)
(*lit: to use the
pederast's entrance*)

Fellatio, a blow-job, a bit of French . . .

FRENCH

Le coit buccal (le cwah book-ahl)
(*lit: mouth-fucking*)

Veux-tu laver les dents? (vi-too lavvay lay dong?)
(*lit: would you like to wash your teeth?*)

Taillage de plume (ty-yahj de ploom)
(*lit: sharpening a pencil*)

Faire comme une pipe (fayr comm oon peep)
(*lit: make like smoking a pipe*)

Souffler dans la canne (sooflay dong la cann)
(*lit: blowing in the cane*)

GERMAN

Fellatio (Fellahtyo)
(*lit: fellatio*)

Ein Französisch (eyen Frantzosich)
(*lit: a French*)

SPANISH

Il sexo oralmente (eel sexo oralmen-tay)
(*lit: oral sex*)

ITALIAN

Una pompa (oona pompa)
(*lit: a pump*)

Un boccione (oon botch-oh-nay)
(*lit: a mouth-job*)

PORTUGUESE

O sexo bucal
(*lit: mouth-sex*)

Fellatio, a blow-job, a bit of French . . . cont.

FRENCH

Prendre en poire
(prond-r ong pwar)
(*colloq: to take in the
face*)

Between the sheets, bedroom conversation . . .

FRENCH	GERMAN	SPANISH
Nous bourriquons à gogo (noo boorikons ah gogo) (*colloq: we make love wildly*)	Ein Kuß (eyen Kuss) (*lit: a kiss*)	Nunca he vista polla tamena (noonkah hay vees-tah poll-yah tah-may-nah) (*lit: I've never seen such an enormous bird, cock*)
Jus de cyclope (shew de seeklop) (*lit: juice of the cyclops, the one-eyed monster, semen*)	Orgasmus (*lit: orgasm*)	
	Orgastich (orgasteek) (*lit: orgiastic*)	Bragas (*colloq: panties*)
Doudounes (doodoon) (*colloq: breasts, tits*)	Cunnilingus (*lit: cunnilingus*)	¿Te duele? (tay doo-ay-lay?) (*lit: does it hurt?*)
	Samenflüssigkeit (sarmenfloosigkite) (*colloq: semen*)	

ITALIAN

Succhiata la figa
(soo-kee-ah-tah la
fee-gah)
(*lit: to suck the
vagina, cunnilingus*)

Un bacio (oon
batcho)
(*lit: a kiss*)

Orgasmo
(*lit: orgasm*)

Sperma
(*lit: sperm*)

PORTUGUESE

Um beijo (oom
bayshoo)
(*lit: a kiss*)

Amavir (ahmaveer)
(*lit: seduction*)

Le parte superior (ley
partay soopayrayohr)
(*lit: the main portion,
the breasts*)

Têta (taytah)
(*colloq: breasts, tits*)

Between the sheets, bedroom conversation . . . cont.

FRENCH

Connais-tu l'histoire de chou? (cohnay-too leestwaar de shoo?) (*lit: do you know the story of the cabbage, the birds and the bees?*)

Brouter de cresson (broo-tay de cressong) (*lit: to graze on the watercress, cunnilingus*)

Bouffer la chatte (boofay la shat) (*lit: to eat the pussy, cunnilingus*)

J'ai le six heures de l'alcoolique (j'ay le see-zur de lah-ko-hol-leek) (*colloq: I've got brewer's droop*)

GERMAN

Sperma (*lit: sperm*)

SPANISH

Un beso (oon baysoh) (*lit: a kiss*)

ITALIAN

È grande come una casa (eh gran-day cohmay oo-na cah-sa) (*lit: it's as big as a house*)

Tesoro (tesoh-roh) (*colloq: darling*)

Cocca (kotcha) (*colloq: my love, my pet*)

Piccola, piccolo, piccina (peekolah, peekoloh, pee-ki-nah) (*colloq: my little one, endearments*)

Frottage (frot-tah-jay) (*colloq: to rub slowly up against*)

Apri a me (*lit: open to me*)

PORTUGUESE

Imbuir, impregnar (armbooeer, armpraynar) (*colloq: to penetrate, to enter*)

Espermacete (eshpayrmashetay) (*lit: sperm*)

Between the sheets, bedroom conversation . . . cont.

FRENCH

Baiser lingual
(bay-zay leeng-gwall)
(*lit: a lingual fuck, a French kiss*)

Balancer la purée
(bah-long-say la pewray)
(*lit: to chuck out the purée, to orgasm*)

ITALIAN

Piange per te
(pee-ahn-jay per tay)
(*lit: it cries for you,
I'm coming*)

Dai! (die!)
(*lit: come on!*)

Piano, piano (pee-ah-
noh, pee-ah-noh)
(*lit: slowly, slowly*)

BEFORE, DURING (AND AFTER) THE MATCH

BEFORE, DURING (AND AFTER) THE MATCH

The match . . .

FRENCH

Où est la partie? (oo eh la partee?)
(*lit: where is the game?*)

Où en est la partie? (oo en eh la partee?)
(*lit: what's the score?*)

Une balle en courbe (oon bahl ong coorb)
(*lit: a curving ball, a banana shot*)

Veinard! (veyn-yar!)
(*colloq: lucky sod!*)

On aurait de gagner mais on a tout loupé (on oh-ray de gahn-yay mez-on a too loo-pay)

GERMAN

Wo ist der Fußball? (vo ist der foossball?)
(*lit: where is the football?*)

Wie steht's? (vee stehts?)
(*lit: what's the position, the score?*)

Leicht! (lie-kt!)
(*lit: easy*)

Wir waren bestohlen worden! (veer vaaren bestohlen voorden!)
(*lit: we was robbed!*)

Glück gehabt! (glook gehabt!)
(*colloq: lucky sods!*)

SPANISH

¿Donde el partido? (donday ell par-tee-doh?)
(*lit: where's the match?*)

Bálon (bah-lone)
(*lit: football*)

¡Barbero! (bar-bay-roh!)
(*colloq: great! good shot!*)

Es un tio barbero (es oon tee-oh bar-bay-roh)
(*colloq: he's a hell of a player, man*)

Sacer (sas-sayr)
(*colloq: kick-off*)

ITALIAN

Dov'é il calcio?
(dohvay eel kal-
choh?)
(*lit: where is the
football match?*)

Qual'è il punteggio?
(kwal-eh eel poon-
tedge-oh?)
(*lit: what's the score?*)

Un goal!
(*lit: goal!*)

Facile! (fatcheelay!)
(*lit: easy!*)

Un' rompi scatole
(oon rompy skatolay)
(*lit: a box-breaker, a
hard player*)

PORTUGUESE

Onde é o futebol?
(onday eh oh
footboll?)
(*lit: where is the
football match?*)

Qual é o resultado?
(kahl eh oh
reshooltahdoh?)
(*lit: what's the score?*)

DUTCH

War is het voetbal?
(var is het vote-bahl?)
(*lit: where is the
football?*)

Wat is de stand?
(*lit: what is the
score?*)

The match . . . cont.

FRENCH

(*lit: we should have
won but we missed
too many chances*)

Il est le resort de
la machine (eel
eh le raysor de la
mah-sheen)
(*lit: he's the brains,
the focus of the team*)

Avec les doigts dans
le nez (avek lay dwa
dong le neh)
(*lit: with our fingers
up our nose, easy!*)

Il joue ramollo (eel
shew ramolloh)
(*lit: he plays softly,
he plays like a fairy*)

SPANISH

¡Que lastima! (kay
lass-tee-mah!)
(*colloq: outrageous,
bad decision!*)

Eso una tramp
(*colloq: it's a fix!*)

ITALIAN

Un' rompi coglioni
(oon rompy coll-ye-
ownay)
(*lit: a ball-breaker, a
hard player*)

Che culo! (kay kooloh!)
(*lit: what arse! what
luck!*)

Che figa! (kay fika!)
(*lit: what cunt! what
luck!*)

Bestiale! (besti-ahlay!)
(*colloq: wild,
exciting!*)

Mio stufo, mio
scocciato (meeoh
stoofoh, meeoh
skotch-ahtoh)
(*colloq: I'm fed up,
disappointed, sick as
a parrot*)

Do you want a fight? A dandruff sandwich? A bunch of fives . . .?

FRENCH

Veux-tu une bagarre?
(vi-too oon bag-arr?)
(*lit: do you want a
fight?*)

Je veux abîmer le
portrait à . . . (je vis
abeemay le portrayt
ah . . .)
(*lit: I want to spoil
the picture of . . ., I
want to push . . .'s
face in*)

Battre . . . comme
plâtre (batt-r . . .
coom plaht-r)
(*lit: to beat up . . .
like plaster, to
smash . . . to pieces*)

GERMAN

Wollen Sie der
Kampf? (vollen see
der Kampf?)
(*lit: do you want a
fight?*)

Er will jemanden
aufmischen (er
vill yaymanden
owfmisken)
(*lit: I want to mix
someone up*)

SPANISH

¿Quiere una pelea?
(kee-ay-ree oona
pel-laya?)
(*lit: do you want a
fight?*)

Si esta víbora te pica,
no hay remedio en
la botica (see estah
vee-bora tay peeca,
no hay re-may-dee-oh
en la bo-tee-ca)
(*lit: if this snake
bites you, there's
no remedy at the
chemist, you're
playing with fire*)

Meterse entre las
patas de los caballos
(met-ersay entray
las patass de loss
caball-yoss)

ITALIAN

Cosa vuole? Una lite?
(cosa vwoh-lay? oona
leetay?)
(*lit: what do you
want? a fight?*)

Vuole un
combattimento
al'ultimo sangue?
(vwoh-lay oon
com-battee-mentoh
al'oolteemoh sang-
gway?)
(*lit: do you want a
fight to the last blood,
to death?*)

Ha lottato con le
unghie e con i denti
(ah lot-tahtoh con lay
cong-gay eh con ee
den-tee)
(*lit: he fought tooth
and nail*)

GREEK

Thelis enas ayonas?
(*lit: do you want a
fight?*)

PORTUGUESE

O que deseja? Uma
discussão? (Oh kay
deshay-ya? Ooma
dishcooshow?)
(*lit: do you want to
argue?*)

DUTCH

Heb je zin in een
gevecht? (heb ye shin
in een het gev-ekt?
(*lit: are you looking
for a fight?*)

Do you want a fight? A dandruff sandwich? A bunch of fives . . .? cont.

FRENCH

Casser la gueule
à . . . (cassay la ghoul
ah . . .)
(*lit: to break the jaw
of . . .*)

Toi et qui encore?
(twa eh key ongkor?)
(*lit: you and who
else? you and whose
army?*)

Se foutre sur la
gueule (se foot-r
sewer la ghoul)
(*lit: to stick one on
the mouth; very rude*)

SPANISH

(*lit: to get in among
the horses' feet, to get
stuck in*)

Luchamos con todas
nuestras fuerzas
(loochahmoss conn
toddass nooehstrass
fuerthass)
(*lit: we fought with
all our force, we went
at them hammer and
tongs*)

Luchamos a brazo
partido (loochahmoss
ah brath-oh parteedo)
(*lit: we struggled until
our strength left, we
fought tooth and nail*)

¡Pegale! (pay-gah-lay!)
(*lit: hit him!*)

ITALIAN

Quei due stanno
facendo di tutto
per venire alle mani
(kway-ee doo-ay
stan-noh fatchendoh
dee too-toh per
ven-ee-ray allay
mah-nee)
(*lit: those two are
spoiling for a fight*)

Do you want a fight? A dandruff sandwich? A bunch of fives . . .? cont.

SPANISH

Armar un jaleo
(armarr oon ha-lay-
oh)
(*colloq: to kick up a
row*)

Se llevó una paliza
tremenda (sail yehvoh
oona pah-leeth-ah
tray-mendah)
(*lit: he got a bad
cudgelling*)

¡Chupate esa!
(choo-pahtay ehsa!)
(*lit: suck on that! take
that!*)

Go away, get lost, sod off, beat it . . .

FRENCH

Va t'en! (va tong!)
(*lit: beat it!*)

Foutre le camp!
(Foot-r le cohm!)
(*lit: fuck off!*)

De l'air! (de lerr!)
(*lit: get to the air,
disappear!*)

Débarrasse! (day-
barrass!)
(*colloq: clear off!*)

Va au diable! (vah oh
dee-ahbl!)
(*lit: go to the devil!*)

Faire une crasse
à . . . (fayr oon crass
ah . . .)
(*colloq: to give the
finger to . . .*)

GERMAN

Gehen Sie weg!
(gayhen see veg!)
(*lit: go away!*)

Geh' weg! (gay veg!)
(*colloq: get lost!*)

Verpiß Dich!
(verpeesh deek!)
(*lit: piss off!*)

Sieh zu, daß Du
Land gewinnst! (see
tzoo, dass doo landt
gevinst!)
(*lit: see you, get some
land covered, get out
of here!*)

Geh' zum Teufel!
(gay tzoom Toyfell!)
(*lit: go to the devil!*)

SPANISH

¡Vete a bañar! (vaytay
a bayn-yar!)
(*lit: go take a bath!*)

¡Vete a ver si ya puso
la cochina! (vaytay a
vayr see ya poosoh la
cotcheenah!)
(*lit: go see if the pig
has laid an egg!*)

¡Vayase! (vayahzee!)
(*colloq: get lost!*)

¡Vete a echar pulgas
a otre parte! (vaytay
ah etcharr poolgass
ah ohtray partay!
(*lit: go and give your
fleas to someone else!*)

¡Que va! (kay vah!)
(*colloq: go on!*)

ITALIAN

Vattene! (vat-tay-nay!)
(*colloq: get lost!*)

Va farti fottere! (va fartee fot-tay-ray!)
(*lit: go and get stuffed!*)

Va fa'nculo! (va fahn-coo-loh!)
(*colloq: stick it up your arse!*)

Va al'inferno! (va ah leen-fayr-noh!)
(*lit: go to hell!*)

Va cagare! (va ca-ga-ray!)
(*lit: go take a shit!*)

Fila via! (feela vee-ah!)
(*colloq: get out of here!*)

GREEK

Fiye!
(*lit: get away!*)

PORTUGUESE

Ordeno-lhe que saia! (ordaynoh-lay kay saya!)
(*lit: I order you to leave!*)

Vá-se embora! (vah-shay emborah!)
(*colloq: get lost!*)

Vá para o diabo! (vah para o dee-ah-boh!)
(*lit: go to hell!*)

DUTCH

Ga weg! (ga vek!)
(*colloq: beat it!*)

Go away, get lost, sod off, beat it . . . cont.

FRENCH

Va te faire foutre!
(vah te fayr foot-r!)
(*lit: go fuck yourself!*)

GERMAN

Verschwinde!
(vayrshvindeh!)
(*colloq: disappear!*)

The police, the old bill . . .

FRENCH

La police
(*lit: the police*)

La bourrique (la
booreek)
(*colloq: the donkeys*)

Les flics (lay fleek)
(*colloq: the cops*)

GERMAN

Die Polizei (dye
pollits-eye)
(*lit: the police*)

Die Bullen (dye
boolen)
(*colloq: the bulls*)

SPANISH

La policía (lah
polee-thee-ah)
(*lit: the police*)

ITALIAN

Ma va la!
(*colloq: get away!*)

Ma dai! (ma die!)
(*colloq: go on!*)

DUTCH

Loop naar de maan
(lohp nar du mahn)
(*colloq: go to hell!*)

ITALIAN

La polizia (lah
polit-sia)
(*lit: the police*)

La polla (lah pohl-
lah)
(*colloq: the chickens,
abbrev. of polizia*)

GREEK

I astinomia
(*lit: the police*)

PORTUGUESE

Um policia (oom
poleeshia)
(*lit: the police*)

DUTCH

De politie (de
politee)
(*lit: the police*)

STRAIGHT TALKING
(HOW TO LOSE FRIENDS AND INFLUENCE PEOPLE)

STRAIGHT TALKING (HOW TO LOSE FRIENDS AND INFLUENCE

Damn, blast, shit and buggeration! . . .

FRENCH

Zut! (zoot!)
(*colloq: blast!*)

Sacrebleu! (sakri-bli!)
(*colloq: holy cow!*)

Nom d'un chien!
(nom dun shang!)
(*lit: name of a dog!*)

Sacristi! (sakreess-
tee!)
(*colloq: damn!*)

Merde! (mair-d!)
(*lit: shit!*)

GERMAN

Verdammt!
(*lit: damn!*)

Verflixt!
(*colloq: blast!*)

Scheiße! (shy-seh!)
(*lit: shit!*)

Verdammte Scheiße!
(verdamt shy-seh!)
(*lit: damn and shit!*)

SPANISH

¡Maldición! (mal-
deeth-ee-ohn!)
(*colloq: damnation!*)

¡Maldita sea!
(mal-deeta sayah!)
(*colloq: damn it all!*)

Soltar un terno
(*lit: to offer a curse*)

¡Mierda! (mee-ayr-
dah!)
(*lit: shit!*)

¡Por Dios! (por
dee-oss!)
(*lit: for God's sake!*)

¡Joder! (hoh-dayr!)
(*lit: fuck!*)

PEOPLE)

Damn, blast, shit and buggeration! . . . cont.

ITALIAN

Dio boia! (deeoh boya!)
(*lit: God's executioner!*)

Merde! (mayr-day!)
(*lit: shit!*)

Che seccatura! (kay seka-too-rah!)
(*colloq: what a barren scene, what a piss-off!*)

Porco Dio! (porkoh deeoh!)
(*lit: swine God!*)

Porco cane! (porkoh cah-nay!)
(*lit: swine dog!*)

GREEK

Na pari i oryi!
(*colloq: for Heaven's sake!*)

PORTUGUESE

Raios me partam!
(rayosh me partam!)
(*colloq: damn me!*)

Bolas! (bohlash!)
(*lit: balls!*)

Merda!
(*lit: shit!*)

Oh diabo! (oh dee-ah-boh!)
(*lit: hell!*)

Damn, blast, shit and buggeration! . . . cont.

SPANISH

¡Puñeta! (poon-yeh-tah!)
(*lit: hell!*)

ITALIAN

Dio cane! (deeoh
cah-nay!)
(*lit: God dog!*)

Dio bueno! (deeoh
bway-noh!)
(*lit: good God!*)

Per la miseria!
(perlah meez-air-ee-
ah!)
(*colloq: for the
misery, for Christ's
sake!*)

Per la Madonna
(*lit: for the Madonna,
for the love of God!*)

DUTCH

Verdikkeme!
(verdikoomoo!)
(*colloq: damn, blast!*)

Verdomme!
(*colloq: damn!*)

Bloody great! Ace! Fantastic! . . .

FRENCH

Fiston! Vas-y!
(feestohng! Vaz-zee!)
(*colloq: attaboy!*)

Formidable! (for-mee-
dahb-l!)
(*colloq: excellent!*)

De première! (de
pray-mee-air!)
(*lit: the best!*)

Terrible! (ter-reeb-l!)
(*colloq: bad! wild!*)

À tout casser! (a too
cassay!)
(*lit: it beats all!*)

Ça baigne dans l'huile
(sah behnyeh dong
l'eweel)
(*lit: it's bathing in oil,
it's smooth, it's good*)

Génial (jayn-yall)
(*colloq: cool*)

GERMAN

Das ist toll! (das ist
tohl!
(*colloq: superb!*)

Hervorragend!
(*colloq: excellent!*)

Großartig! (groshartik!)
(*colloq: fantastic!*)

SPANISH

No habrá problema
(no ahbrah prob-lay-
mah)
(*colloq: no sweat!*)

¡Cojonudo! (coc-
honoo-doh!)
(*colloq: great balls!
excellent!*)

¡Barbaro!
(*colloq: wild! great!*)

¡Estupendo! (ess-too-
pen-doh!)
(*lit: stupendous!*)

¡Magnifico! (mag-
neefeecoh!)
(*lit: magnificent!*)

Bloody great! Ace! Fantastic! . . . cont.

ITALIAN

Bestiale! (bes-tee-ah-
lay!)
(*lit: wild! great!*)

Omocidiale! (oh-moh-
cheedi-ah-lay!)
(*lit: murderous!
killer!*)

Che culo! (kay
kooloh!)
(*lit: what arse! what
luck!*)

Stupendo!
(stoopendoh!)
(*lit: stupendous!*)

Fantastico!
(fantasteekoh!)
(*lit: fantastic!*)

Superbo! (soo-payr-
boh!)
(*lit: superb!*)

GREEK

Iperoha!
(*colloq: great!*)

Fadastikos!
(*lit: fantastic!*)

Katapliktikos!
(*colloq: brilliant!*)

PORTUGUESE

Isso é optimo! (eesho
eh opteemoh!)
(*lit: that's the best!*)

Brilhante! (breelanteh!)
(*lit: brilliant!*)

Fantástico!
(fantasteekoh!)
(*lit: fantastic!*)

DUTCH

Das is fantastisch!
(das is fantasteesh!)
(*lit: that is fantastic!*)

Prachtig! (prashtug!)
(*colloq: wonderful!*)

Voortreffelijk!
(voortreffellook!)
(*colloq: unbeatable!*)

You absolute bastard, and other common, garden and mortal insults . . .

FRENCH

Tu peux te le mettre au cul! (too pi te le mett-r oh coo!)
(*lit: stick it up your arse!*)

Tête de veau! (teht de voh!)
(*lit: veal-head! Baldie!*)

Salaud! (sal-loh!)
(*colloq: you bastard!*)

Vaurien! (vohreeang!)
(*colloq: you useless bastard!*)

Sale vicelard! (sahl veess-eh-larh!)
(*colloq: you dirty sod!*)

GERMAN

Du Depp!
(*lit: you moron!*)

Du Idiot!
(*lit: you idiot!*)

Du Arschloch!
(*lit: you arsehole!*)

Dumme Sau!
(dummeh sow!)
(*lit: stupid sow!*)

Lahmarsch!
(*lit: slow-arse!*)

Arschficker!
(*lit: arse-fucker!*)

Du Penner!
(*lit: you tramp!*)

SPANISH

¡Imbêcil! (imbeceel!)
(*lit: imbecile!*)

¡Flaco! (flahkoh!)
(*lit: skinny sod!*)

¡Gordo! (gordoh!)
(*lit: fat bastard!*)

¡Pequeño y gordo! (pay-ken-yo ee gordo!)
(*lit: short fat bastard!*)

¡Que asco! (kay askoh!)
(*lit: how disgusting!*)

Es un barbero (ess oon bar-bay-roh)
(*colloq: he sucks up to beards, he's an arse-licker*)

ITALIAN

Furfante! (foorfantay!)
(*colloq: scoundrel!*)

Uno sciocco (oono
shock-oh)
(*lit: a fool*)

Capra stupido! (kapra
stoo-peedoh!)
(*lit: stupid goat!*)

Fai la figura d'un
allocco (fie la
fee-goo-rah doon
al-loc-oh)
(*lit: you look like an
idiot*)

Asino! (aseenoh!)
(*lit: donkey!*)

GREEK

Enas anoitos!
(*colloq: that fool!*)

Nothos!
(*lit: bastard!*)

Goorooni vlakia!
(*colloq: ignorant pig!*)

PORTUGUESE

Tu besuntāo! (too
bayshuntow!)
(*colloq: you dirty
bastard!*)

Tu velhaco! (too
vayl-ahkoh!)
(*colloq: you lying
sod!*)

You absolute bastard, and other common, garden and mortal insults . . . cont.

FRENCH

Une mauvaise graine
(oon mow-vayz gren)
(*lit: a bad seed, a
nasty piece of work*)

Une vieille bique
(oon vyai beek)
(*colloq: an old bat*)

Espèce de frepouille!
(ess-pess de freh-
pwee-yeh!)
(*lit: scoundrel!*)

Espèce de maladroit!
(ess-pess de mallah-
drwa!)
(*lit: you clumsy sod!*)

Bon sang d'imbecile!
(bon song dam-bee-
seel!)
(*lit: blood of an
imbecile! you bloody
fool!*)

SPANISH

No digas tonterias
(noh deegass ton-tay-
ree-ass)
(*colloq: don't talk
rubbish*)

Esta un vago (estah
oon vahgoh)
(*lit: he is a bum, a
layabout*)

¡Mugre! (moog-ray!)
(*lit: you filth!*)

¡Esta muy pedante!
(estah mwee pay-
dantay!)
(*colloq: he's a
conceited oaf!*)

¡Hijo de puta!
(eek-ho de pootah!)
(*lit: son of a whore,
son of a bitch!*)

ITALIAN

Ne ho fin sopra
i capelli de te (nay
aw feen sop-rah ee
capelli day tay)
(*lit: I'm up to the
hair with you, I'm
fed up with you*)

Sia brutta come la
fame (see-ah brootah
coh-may la fahmay)
(*lit: she's as ugly as a
famine, she's ugly as
sin*)

Lui è brutto da morire
(loo-ee brootoh da
morreeray)
(*lit: he's as ugly as
death*)

Testardo! (tays-tar-
doh!)
(*colloq: stubborn get!*)

PORTUGUESE

Tu biltre! (too
beel-tray!)
(*colloq: you rascal!*)

Um fulano (oom
foolahnoh)
(*colloq: an
untrustworthy
bugger*)

Bucha! (boosha!)
(*colloq: fat fool!*)

Idiota! (idioh-tah!)
(*lit: idiot!*)

Cabrâo! (kabrow!)
(*colloq: bastard!*)

Cabrona! (kabrohnah!)
(*colloq: bad bastard!*)

You absolute bastard, and other common, garden and mortal insults . . . cont.

FRENCH

Espèce de couillon!
(ess-pess de cwee-
yong!)
(lit: *you silly bugger!*)

Un vrai gugusse (oon
vray gu-goose)
(colloq: *a silly twat!*)

Un vieux gaga (uhn
vyou gaga)
(colloq: *an old fool*)

Sale petite lope! (sahl
peteet lowp!)
(colloq: *you dirty
little bugger!*)

SPANISH

Cachigo dete
(ka-cheegoh daytay)
(colloq: *short-arse*)

¡Pendejo! (payndek-
ho!)
(lit: *you pubic hair!*)

¡Cabrón! (kabrohn!)
(lit: *billy-goat*)
(colloq: *cuckold! – a*
serious *insult*)

¡Me cago en la leche
de tu puta madre!
(me cah-goh en
lah lay-chay de too
pootah mahdray!)
(lit: *I shit in the
milk of your whoring
mother! – a* mortal
insult!)

ITALIAN

Vecchio porco!
(vek-kee-oh porko!)
(*lit: old pig!*)

Uno scemo (oono
skaymoh)
(*lit: an idiot*)

Bastardo! (bastardoh!)
(*lit: bastard!*)

Stronzo! stront-soh!)
(*lit: turd!*)

Testa di cazzo!
(taystah dee catsoh!)
(*lit: dickhead!*)

Figlio di putana!
(feel-yoh dee
pootahnah!
(*lit: son of a whore!*)

You absolute bastard, and other common, garden and mortal insults . . . cont.

He is crazy, he's off his rocker, he's two eggs short of a dozen . . .

FRENCH

Il est fou (eel eh foo)
(*lit: he is crazy*)

Elle a une araignée
au plafond (ell ah
oon arrayn-yay oh
plahfon)
(*lit: she has a spider
on the ceiling*)

Il est dingo (eel eh
dang-go)
(*colloq: he's daft*)

GERMAN

Er ist verrückt (er ist
verrookt)
(*lit: he's crazy*)

Er ist ein Idiot
(*lit: he is an idiot*)

SPANISH

Se loco (say lohkoh)
(*lit: he is mad*)

Le patina el coco (lay
pateenah el coco)
(*lit: his coconut has
slipped*)

Se con delirio (say on
day-lee-ri-oh)
(*lit: he's delirious,
he's nuts*)

ITALIAN

Maladetto fottuto!
(mala-day-toh
fot-tootoh!)
(*colloq: damned
idiot!*)

ITALIAN

Lui è pazzo (loo-ee
eh patso)
(*lit: he is crazy*)

È rimbambito (eh
reem-bam-beetoh)
(*colloq: he's dizzy,
scatty, foolish*)

Ha la testa nelle
nuvole (ah la tays-tah
nellay noo-volay)
(*colloq: she's got her
head in the clouds*)

GREEK

Ine trelos
(*lit: he's crazy*)

PORTUGUESE

Está doido (eshtah
doydoh)
(*lit: he's bonkers*)

Está louco (eshtah
looco)
(*lit: he's loco*)

He is crazy, he's off his rocker, he's two eggs short of a dozen . . . cont.

FRENCH

Il a onduler de
la toiture (eel ah
ondoolay de la
twa-toor)
(*lit: he has a shaky
roof, he has a screw
loose*)

Elle a une chauve-
souris dans le
beffroi (ell ah oon
showv-sooree dong le
beffrwa)
(*lit: she has a bat in
the belfry*)

SPANISH

Se más loco que
una cabra (say maas
lohkoh kay oona
kabrah)
(*lit: he's crazier than
a goat*)

Se loco de remate
(say lohkoh day
ray-mah-tay)
(*colloq: he's stark
raving mad*)

Faltarle a uno un
tornillo (fal-tar-
lay a oono oon
torr-neel-yoh)
(*colloq: to have a
screw loose*)

Se volvió loco (say
vohlveeoh lohkoh)
(*lit: he went crazy*)

ITALIAN

Passesco! (passeskoh!)
(*colloq: that's crazy!*)

È fuori di testa (eh
fwoh-ree dee tays-tah)
(*lit: he's off his head*)

È matto (eh maht-
toh)
(*lit: he's mad*)

PORTUGUESE

Está lunático (eshtah
loonah-teecoh)
(*lit: he's mad*)

Está tonto (eshtah
tontoh)
(*lit: he's off his head*)

DUTCH

Hij is gek (he is gek)
(*lit: he is mad*)

Está demente (eshtah
daymentay)
(*lit: he's demented*)

Está desequilibrado
(eshtah day-sekee-lee-
brah-doh)
(*colloq: he's unhinged*)

He is crazy, he's off his rocker, he's two eggs short of a dozen . . . cont.

SPANISH

Esta loco de atar
(esta lohkoh day atar)
(*lit: he's completely
beside himself*)

And finally, a fart, a raspberry, a Bronx cheer . . .

FRENCH

Un pet (uhn payt)
(*colloq: a fart*)

Une pastille (oon
pastee)
(*lit: a small, sweet-
smelling confectionery*)

Une perle (oon perl)
(*lit: a pearl*)

Une loffe (oon loff)
(*colloq: a fart*)

GERMAN

Ein furtzen (eyen
foortsen)
(*lit: a fart*)

Einen fahren lassen
(eyenen fahren
lassen)
(*lit: to let one go, to
drive one out*)

SPANISH

Un fallón (oon
fallohn)
(*lit: a noiseless rocket*)

Un peer (oon peer)
(*colloq: a fart*)

Un pedo (oon
paydoh)
(*colloq: a fart*)

Un pedorro (oon
paydor-roh)
(*colloq: a frequent
farter*)

ITALIAN

Un peto (oon paytoh)
(*colloq: a fart*)

Una scoreggia (oona
skoredge-ah)
(*colloq: a big fart*)